KIDS ON EARTH

Wildlife Adventures – Explore The World
Squirrel Monkey - Costa Rica

Sensei Paul David

COPYRIGHT PAGE

Kids On Earth: Wildlife Adventures - Explore The World

Squirrel Monkey - Costa Rica

by Sensei Paul David,

Copyright © 2023.

All rights reserved.

978-1-77848-165-9 KoE_WildLife_Amazon_PaperbackBook_costarica_squirrel monkey

978-1-77848-164-2 KoE_WildLife_Amazon_eBook_costarica_squirrel monkey

978-1-77848-414-8 koe_wildlife_ingram_paperbackbook_squirrelmonkey

This book is not authorized for free distribution copying.

www.senseipublishing.com

@senseipublishing
#senseipublishing

Synopsis

This book provides 30 unique and fun facts about the Squirrel Monkey, a species of primate found in the tropical rainforests of Central and South America, including Costa Rica. It explores their diet, behavior, habitat, and social structure. It also covers their special features, such as their curved claws, large eyes, and long tails. The book also explains why these primates make great pets and why they are important to the rainforest ecosystem. Whether you are 6 or 12, you will find something fascinating about the Squirrel Monkey!

Get Our FREE Books Now!

kidsonearth.life

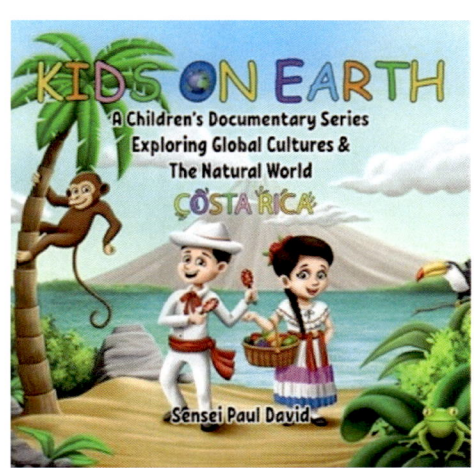

kidsonearth.world

Click Below for Another Book In Each Series

senseipublishing.com/KoE_SERIES

senseipublishing.com/KoE_Wildlife_SERIES

KoE En Español

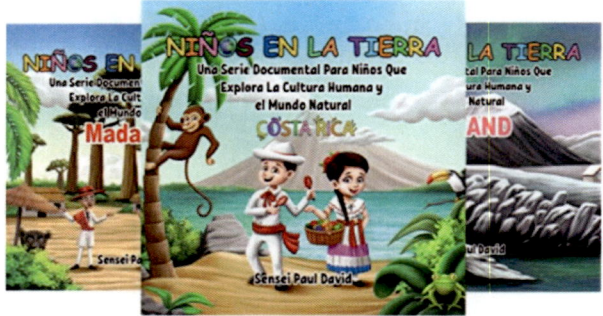

senseipublishing.com/KoE_SERIES_SPANISH

www.senseipublishing.com

Join Our Publishing Journey!

If you would like to receive FUTURE FREE BOOKS and get to know us better, please click www.senseipublishing.com and join our newsletter by entering your email address in the pop-up box.

Follow Our Blog: senseipauldavid.ca

Follow/Like/Subscribe: Facebook, Instagram, YouTube: @senseipublishing

Scan the QR Code with your phone or tablet to follow us on social media:

Like / Subscribe / Follow

Introduction

Welcome to the world of the amazing Squirrel Monkey! This book is full of amazing fun facts about these incredible creatures. From their unique diet to their fascinating behavior, you will learn all about their lives in the rainforest of Costa Rica. You will explore their natural habitat and discover why they make such great pets. No matter your age, you will find something fascinating about these incredible creatures. So read on and explore the world of the Squirrel Monkey!

Squirrel Monkeys are found in the tropical rainforests of Central and South America, including Costa Rica.

These primates have a diet that includes fruits, nuts, and insects.

They have curved claws on their hands and feet that help them climb trees quickly.

Squirrel Monkeys are very social animals and live in large groups of up to 200 individuals.

They have large eyes, which allow them to see in the dark.

Squirrel Monkeys have a variety of colorful pelts, including yellow, orange, and black.

These primates can leap up to 8 feet in the air!

Squirrel Monkeys are very vocal and make a variety of different sounds.

They are omnivores and eat both plants and animals.

Squirrel Monkeys are excellent swimmers and can often be seen playing in the water.

They use their long tails to hang from branches and help them balance.

Squirrel Monkeys are very intelligent and can be trained to do tricks.

These primates have a lifespan of up to 15 years in the wild.

Squirrel Monkeys are diurnal, meaning they are active during the day and sleep at night.

They have a unique mating system, with each male mating with multiple females.

These primates live in the treetops and rarely come down to the ground.

Squirrel Monkeys have a special bonding behavior with their mothers, which is known as "babysitting".

They communicate with each other using a variety of facial expressions and body language.

These primates are very playful and enjoy playing with each other and their environment.

Squirrel Monkeys have a wide array of predators, including snakes, hawks, and even cats!

They are also very territorial and are known to fight with intruders.

Squirrel Monkeys have a loud call that can be heard up to a mile away.

These primates are excellent climbers and can climb up to 30 feet in a single bound!

Their tails are used to grab branches and help them move through the canopy.

Squirrel Monkeys are very curious and will often explore their surroundings.

They have a unique digestive system that helps them to extract nutrients from their food.

These primates are sometimes kept as pets but require a lot of care and attention.

Squirrel Monkeys are important to the rainforest ecosystem, as they help to spread the seeds of the plants they eat.

They have a unique ability to adapt to their environment, allowing them to survive in many different habitats.

Squirrel Monkeys are some of the most fascinating creatures in the world and are truly amazing to watch in the wild.

Conclusion

The Squirrel Monkey is an incredibly interesting creature, with a unique diet and behavior that sets them apart from other primates. They are intelligent, social, and very curious animals that are a joy to watch in the wild. They are also important to the rainforest ecosystem, as they help to spread the seeds of the plants they eat. No matter your age, you will find something fascinating about the Squirrel Monkey!

Thank you for reading this book!

If you found this book helpful, I would be grateful if you would **post an honest review on Amazon** so this book can reach other supportive readers like you!

All you need to do is digitally flip to the back and leave your review. Or visit amazon.com/author/senseipauldavid click the correct book cover and click on the blue link next to the yellow stars that say, "customer reviews."

As always…

It's a great day to be alive!

Share Our FREE eBooks Now!

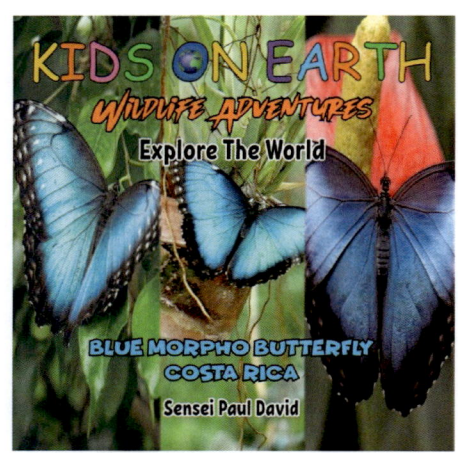

kidsonearth.life

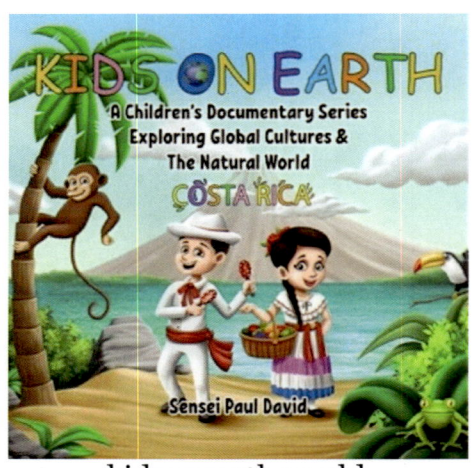

kidsonearth.world

Click Below for Another Book In Each Series

senseipublishing.com/KoE_SERIES

senseipublishing.com/KoE_Wildlife_SERIES

KoE En Español

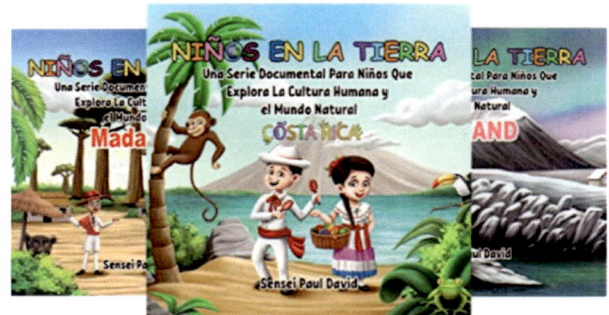

senseipublishing.com/KoE_SERIES_SPANISH

www.senseipublishing.com

Check out our **recommendations** for other books for adults & kids plus other great resources by visiting
www.senseipublishing.com/resources/

Join Our Publishing Journey!

If you would like to receive FREE BOOKS and special offers, please visit www.senseipublishing.com and join our newsletter by entering your email address in the pop-up box

Follow Our Engaging Blog NOW!
senseipauldavid.ca

Get Our FREE Books Today!

Click & Share the Links Below

FREE Kids Books

lifeofbailey.senseipublishing.com

kidsonearth.senseipublishing.com

FREE Self-Development Book

senseiselfdevelopment.senseipublishing.com

FREE BONUS!!!
Experience Over 25 FREE Engaging Guided Meditations!

Prized Skills & Practices for Adults & Kids. Help Restore Deep Sleep, Lower Stress, Improve Posture, Navigate Uncertainty & More.

Download the Free Insight Timer App and click the link below:
http://insig.ht/sensei_paul

About Sensei Publishing

Sensei Publishing commits itself to helping people of all ages transform into better versions of themselves by providing high-quality and research-based self-development books with an emphasis on mental health and guided meditations. Sensei Publishing offers well-written e-books, audiobooks, paperbacks, and online courses that simplify complicated but practical topics in line with its mission to inspire people toward positive transformation.

It's a great day to be alive!

About the Author

I create simple & transformative eBooks & Guided Meditations for Adults & Children proven to help navigate uncertainty, solve niche problems & bring families closer together.

I'm a former finance project manager, private pilot, jiu-jitsu instructor, musician & former University of Toronto Fitness Trainer. I prefer a science-based approach to focus on these & other areas in my life to stay humble & hungry to evolve. I hope you enjoy my work and I'd love to hear your feedback.

- It's a great day to be alive!
Sensei Paul David

Scan & Follow/Like/Subscribe: Facebook, Instagram, YouTube: @senseipublishing

Scan using your phone/iPad camera for Social Media
Visit us at www.senseipublishing.com and sign up for our newsletter to learn more about our exciting books and to experience our FREE Guided Meditations for Kids & Adults.

www.ingramcontent.com/pod-product-compliance
Lightning Source LLC
Chambersburg PA
CBRC090902080526
44587CB00008B/172